Laknavi Kofta Curry

MICROWAVE SUBZIS

TARLA DALAL
India's # 1 Cookery Author

S&C
SANJAY & CO.
MUMBAI

Third Printing : 2010

ISBN: 978-8-189491-37-6

Price: Rs. 89/-

Published & Distributed by : **Sanjay & Company**
353/A-1, Shah & Nahar Industrial Estate, Dhanraj Mill Compound, Lower Parel (W), Mumbai - 400 013. INDIA.
Tel. : (91-22) 4345 2400 • Fax : (91-22) 2496 5876 • E-mail : sanjay@tarladalal.com • Website : www.tarladalal.com

Printed by : Minal Sales Agencies

UK and USA customers can call us on :
UK : 02080029533 • USA : 213-634-1406
For books, Membership on **tarladalal.com**, Subscription for **Cooking & More** and Recipe queries
Timing : 9.30 a.m. to 7.00 p.m. (IST), from Monday to Saturday
Local call charges applicable

Recipe Research & Production Design
Arati Fedane
Umaima Abdulally
Ritika Rajpal
Vibhuti Punjabi

Nutritionists
Nisha Katira
Sapna Kamdar

Food Styling
Shubhangi Dhaimade

Photography
Jignesh Jhaveri

Typesetting
Adityas Enterprises

Designed by
Satyamangal Rege

Copy Editing
Janani Gopalakrishnan

INTRODUCTION

If there is one thing that constrains most people from working wonders in the kitchen in today's quick-paced world, it is '*time*'. The traditional slow cooking practices just do not work well these days because people do not have much time to spend in the kitchen, amidst their multifarious responsibilities at work and home. One device that has defied the clock in the kitchen is the microwave oven. It not only cooks faster but is also very convenient to use. Nowadays even conservative and strictly traditional homes have added the versatile and helpful kitchen helper, to their kitchens.

With a little creativity, several dishes can be prepared using the microwave, not just modern recipes, but traditional ones as well. And if you thought that the use of the microwave was restricted to preparing only western dishes here's a surprise for you it gives me great pleasure to introduce to you, **Microwave Subzis.** A well-planned and comprehensive collection of **40 recipes of delicious Indian subzis** prepared in the microwave. After 3 books like Microwave Cooking, Microwave Snacks & Desserts and Microwave Desi Khana, this is the 4th sequel to the microwave series.

The recipes in the book have been clubbed into five very interesting sections: **Roz ki Subzi, Paneer ki Subzi, Desi Subziyan, Daawatwali Subziyan** and **Swadisht Curries**. They feature a variety of vegetables that are commonly available and also well-suited for microwave cooking. Each recipe has been tested, using 20 litre, 900 watt microwave oven in order to obtain the exact cooking time and provide an unmatched flavour.

However, in order to ensure that every recipe 'works', it is very important that you read the next few pages, which provide some **microwave-cooking tips**.

Another unique feature of this book is the section on **'Basic Cooking Procedures'**, which provides a detailed description of microwave cooking procedures for the vegetables that have been used in the book. These can also be used while you are preparing your own dishes, thus reducing cooking time.

For best results ensure that you refer to the 'Basic Cooking Procedures' section wherever it has been mentioned in the book.

Happy microwave cooking!

CONTENTS

ROZ KI SUBZI

PANEER KI SUBZI

DESI SUBZIYAN

DAWATWALI SUBZIYAN

SWADISHT CURRIES

TIPS FOR USING YOUR MICROWAVE EFFECTIVELY

A microwave oven is like your mixer-grinder or stove or coffee-maker or any other kitchen tool albeit more interesting and versatile. It can do much more, provided you know how to use it safely and effectively. Here are some tips on selecting good utensils for microwave cooking, microwave safety, and basic cooking procedures for various vegetables.

Selecting the right cookware

Certain cookware can be used in the oven and some cannot.

Ovenproof chinaware, glass utensils like those from Borosil, Arcorac etc. and baked pottery dishes (teracotta) are the best choices. Ceramic dishes can also be used provided they are non-porous. To check if the dish is non-porous, heat it in the microwave for 15 to 20 seconds. The dish should not feel warm. Paper plates, towels and 100% cotton and linen napkins can be used only for re-heating and not for cooking. Wood items can be used in the micro-oven but only for short cooking periods. Loose-fitting, microwave-safe lids and microwave-safe cling-wrap can be used, but make sure they have holes in them to allow steam to escape. Shallow and straight dishes work better than deep ones as they ensure faster and uniform cooking.

As to materials that should be avoided, plastics and melamine should not be used for a long time as they cannot withstand the heat emitted by microwaves. Dishes with a sloping base are also to be avoided because they cause the food in the shallow parts to get over-heated and prevent uniform cooking of the food. Similarly deep bowls in which the food gets unevenly distributed and hence unevenly cooked should also be avoided. Metal dishes and foil should not be used while cooking in a microwave. Cookware with golden, silver or metal rims must also be avoided as these may cause arcing. Tight-fitting lids, foils, and metal lids should also be avoided.

Before using any utensil for the first time, carry out this simple test to ascertain whether it is microwave safe. Fill the vessel with approximately 200 ml of water and microwave on HIGH for 2 minutes. If the utensil gets too warm, it should not be used. The water should get heated without heating the vessel.

Do's and don'ts, for microwave safety

The microwave oven's door should never be subject to any strain. So, remember not to bang it, even if you are angry! And avoid opening and closing the door too often. The reason for this is that, even if the door becomes slightly misaligned, it was cause a leakage of microwaves, and hence a loss in the efficiency of the oven. Also, do not operate an empty oven as it will cause damage to it. Leave at least five centimetres space between the back of the oven and the wall, so that there is space for the exhaust air to escape. Avoid installing the oven near gas burners, radios or TVs.

Small quantities of food with low moisture content can burn, spark, or even catch fire if heated for too long. Do not deep fry in the oven as it is not possible to control the temperature of the oil and it may catch fire easily. If food catches fire turn off the oven and remove the plug immediately, but do not open the oven door.

Keep the interior of the oven clean as small specks of food particles inside can reduce its efficiency. Do not cook eggs with the shells as they explode, do not heat food or liquids in bottles with lids closed, and do not warm bottles with lids on for babies.

Milk or any food for kids must be heated on simmer mode only. Pierce vegetables and fruits with tight skin, before cooking them, to prevent them from bursting. Avoid filling dishes to the brim. Dishes must only be ½ or ¾ filled depending on the liquid content of the food. If the dish is too small, the food will boil over and if the dish is too large the thick curry will spread out and overcook. So, choose a proper sized dish depending on the amount of food to be cooked.

Basic cooking procedures, for common ingredients

All the ingredients/vegetables required for cooking an Indian *subzi* can be cooked to perfection in the microwave. Listed below are the methods to cook/boil vegetables that have been used in this book. The cooking time for the ingredients mentioned below have not been included while calculating the preparation or cooking time of the main recipes.

POTATOES

Place 2 whole large potatoes, with the skin, on the microwave turntable. Place a glass of water in the centre to prevent them from getting wrinkled. Microwave on HIGH for 5 minutes till cooked. Remove and peel.

2 large potatoes = ½ cup cooked and mashed potatoes
2 large potatoes = 1 cup cooked and diced potatoes

TOMATOES

Make two light criss-cross slits on 2 large tomatoes and place them in a microwave-safe plate. Microwave on HIGH for 2 minutes. Remove, peel and blend/chop.

2 large tomatoes= ½ cup cooked tomato purée
2 large tomatoes = ½ cup cooked and chopped tomatoes

SPINACH (Palak)

Place 2 cups of chopped spinach in a microwave-proof plate and sprinkle 1 tbsp water on it. Microwave on HIGH for 2 minutes. To make spinach purée, blend the cooked/ blanched spinach in a mixer.

2 cups chopped spinach = 1 cup blanched spinach
1 cup blanched spinach = ¾ cup cooked spinach purée

CORN

Combine 1 cup of corn niblets with ¼ cup of water in a microwave-proof bowl and microwave on HIGH for 5 minutes. Use as required.

GREEN PEAS

Frozen: Place 1 cup frozen peas on a microwave-proof plate. Sprinkle 1 tbsp of water over them and microwave on HIGH for 2 minutes. Use as required.

Fresh: Place 1 cup shelled fresh peas on a microwave proof plate. Sprinkle 2 tbsp of water over them and microwave on HIGH for 5 minutes. Use as required.

Peas purée: Follow any of the above procedure. Allow the peas to cool and blend in a mixer along with enough water to form a thick purée. Use as required.

1 cup cooked green peas = ¾ cup cooked green peas purée

COLOCASIA (Arbi)

Wash 2 cups of colocasia thoroughly and pierce them with a fork. Place them, with the skin, on the microwave turntable. Place a glass of water in the centre to prevent them from getting wrinkled. Microwave on HIGH for 5 minutes till cooked. Remove and peel. Use as required.

Cooking time may vary by 1 to 2 minutes depending on the quality of the colocasia.

MIXED VEGETABLES (CARROTS, CAULIFLOWER, FRENCH BEANS)

Place 1 cup chopped/diced [into 25mm (1″) pieces] vegetables on a microwave-proof plate. Sprinkle 1 tbsp water over them and microwave on HIGH for 3 minutes. Use as required.

The same procedure can be used to cook either 1 cup of the above vegetables individually or 1 cup mixed chopped vegetables.

SPICES AND SEEDS

Place 1 tbsp of the spices/seeds to be roasted, on a microwave-proof plate. Microwave on HIGH for 1 minute. Use as required.

PASTES

For easy and fast microwave cooking it is advisable to always keep a few basic pastes handy in the refrigerator. Here are some pastes that form a part of nearly every Indian *subzi*.

Ginger-garlic paste: Combine ¾ cup of garlic with ¼ cup of ginger and grind along with enough water to make a smooth paste. This should yield 1 cup of ginger-garlic paste (approximately). Store refrigerated in a glass jar and use as required. This paste can be stored in the refrigerator for about 3 weeks.

Onion paste: Roughly chop 3 onions and blend in the mixer along with enough water to make a thick paste. Store refrigerated in a container and use as required. This paste can be stored in the refrigerator for about 2 days.

3 large onions = 1 cup onion paste (approximately)

Green chilli paste: Blend 1 cup of roughly chopped green chillies in a mixer with few drops of lemon juice and enough water to make a thick paste. Lemon juice is added to prevent the green chillies from turning black. Store refrigerated in a container and use as required. This paste can be stored in a bowl in the refrigerator for upto 1 week.

1 cup green chillies = ½ cup green chilli paste (approximately)

Red chilli paste: Soak ½ cup dry red chillies in ¼ cup of water for 15 minutes. Grind to a paste in a mixer along with all the water. Store refrigerated in a container and use as required. This can be stored in a bowl in the refrigerator for upto 1 week.

½ cup dry red chillies = ¼ cup red chilli paste (approximately)

Now that we are set with the basic knowledge about how to use the microwave safely and how to cook the basic ingredients/vegetables, and hopefully also have some handy pastes in the refrigerator, it is time to conjure up some delicious Indian subzis in the microwave!

Note: All the recipes are tried and perfected in a 20 litre, 900 watt microwave oven. The cooking time for the recipes may differ slightly, depending on the size and wattage of your microwave oven.

ROZ KI SUBZI

Chatpata Corn

An unusual and excessively tasty combination of finely crushed groundnuts and crunchy corn niblets, cooked to perfection in the microwave. Easy to whip up and healthy as well, this delectable dish can be had as a snack with bread at any time of the day to satiate those sudden hunger pangs.

Preparation time: 5 to 7 minutes. Cooking time: 5 minutes. Serves 2.

1½ cups cooked corn niblets, refer to page 13
¼ cup finely crushed groundnuts
1 tbsp onion paste
1 tbsp ready-made tomato purée
2 tbsp finely chopped tomatoes
½ tsp finely chopped ginger
½ tsp finely chopped green chillies
A pinch sugar

½ tsp lemon juice
2 tsp oil
Salt to taste

For the garnish
2 tsp finely chopped coriander
2 tsp chopped tomatoes

1. Combine the oil and onion paste in a microwave-proof bowl mix well and microwave on HIGH for 1 minute.
2. Add the groundnuts, tomato purée, tomatoes, ginger, green chillies, sugar, salt and ¼ cup water and mix well microwave on HIGH for 3 minutes.
3. Add the corn niblets, mix well and microwave on HIGH for 1 minute.
4. Add the lemon juice and mix well.
   Serve hot garnished with coriander and tomatoes.

Dahiwale Simla Mirch

Picture on facing page.

Beautifully coloured capsicums in a delightfully tangy gravy, this crunchy subzi is a real treat for the senses.

Preparation time: 10 to 12 minutes. Cooking time: 5 minutes. Serves 2.

¾ cup coloured capsicum cubes
¼ cup cooked and mashed potatoes, refer to page 12
1 tbsp milk
¼ cup curds (*dahi*)
¼ tsp turmeric powder (*haldi*)
½ tsp chilli powder
2 tsp *besan* (Bengal gram flour)
1 tsp cumin seeds (*jeera*)
2 tsp oil
Salt to taste

DAHIWALE SIMLA MIRCH : Recipe above. →

1. Combine the potatoes, milk, curds, turmeric powder, chilli powder, *besan*, salt and ½ cup water in a bowl and mix well to form a smooth mixture. Keep aside.
2. Combine the oil and cumin seeds in microwave-proof bowl, cover with a lid and microwave on HIGH for 1 minute.
3. Add the capsicum, mix well and microwave on HIGH for 1 minute.
4. Add the prepared mixture, mix well and microwave on HIGH for 3 minutes stirring once in between after 1½ minutes.

   Serve hot.

Sukhi Roti ki Subzi

If you are too tired to cook up a meal, and all you have in the refrigerator are some 'sukhi rotis' leftover from last night, don't fret. Here's a mouth-watering subzi made with rotis, tomatoes and a blend of Punjabi spices.

Preparation time: 10 minutes. Cooking time: 2 minutes. Serves 2.

3 rotis, 125 mm. (5") diameter, cut into strips
2 tbsp curds (*dahi*)
¼ tsp turmeric powder (*haldi*)
½ tsp mustard seeds (*rai / sarson*)
½ cumin seeds *(jeera)*
1 tsp chopped green chillies
½ tsp Punjabi *chole masala*
¼ cup chopped tomatoes, lightly mashed
2 tsp oil
Salt to taste

For the garnish
2 tsp chopped coriander

1. Combine the roti, curds, turmeric powder, salt and ¾ cup water in a bowl and mix well. Keep aside for 10 minutes till the roti soaks up the liquid.
2. Combine the oil, mustard seeds, cumin seeds, green chillies in a microwave-proof bowl and microwave on HIGH for 1 minute.
3. Add the soaked roti, Punjabi *chole masala,* tomatoes and salt. Mix well and microwave on HIGH for 1 minute.
   Serve hot garnished with coriander.

Khumbh ki Subzi

Mushrooms in lovely white gravy, mildly flavoured with cardamoms and garam masala. To obtain the right consistency for the gravy make sure that you don't overcook the mushrooms or they will release water and make the gravy bland.

Preparation time: 5 to 7 minutes. Cooking time: 9 minutes. Serves 2.

1 cup sliced mushrooms (*khumbh*)
3 tbsp milk
2 tbsp curds (*dahi*)
½ tsp cornflour
2 cloves (*laung / lavang*)
2 cardamoms (*elaichi*)
½ tsp finely chopped green chillies
¼ tsp chilli powder
¼ tsp *garam masala*
Salt to taste
1 tbsp oil

For the paste
½ cup roughly chopped onions
1 tbsp cashewnuts *(kaju)*
½ tsp ginger-garlic paste

For the garnish
1 tbsp cream

For the paste
1. Combine the onions with ¼ cup of water in a microwave-proof bowl and microwave on HIGH for 4 minutes.
2. Cool and blend to a smooth paste, in a mixer, along with the cashewnuts and ginger-garlic paste. Keep aside.

How to proceed
1. Combine the curds, milk and cornflour in a bowl, mix well and keep aside.
2. Combine the oil, cloves and cardamom in a microwave-proof bowl and microwave on HIGH for 1 minute.
3. Add the prepared paste, green chillies, chilli powder and *garam masala,* mix well and microwave on HIGH for 2 minutes.
4. Add the curds, milk and cornflour mixture, mushrooms and salt, mix well and microwave on HIGH for 2 minutes.

   Serve hot garnished with cream.

Tinda aur Saunf ki Subzi

Eaten with rotis and curds, this easy-to-make and aesthetically seasoned subzi makes for a tasty and balanced meal.

Preparation time: 5 to 7 minutes.   Cooking time: 4 minutes.   Serves 2.

6 *tindas*, peeled and cut into quarters
1 tsp fennel seeds (*saunf*)
½ tsp cumin seeds (*jeera*) powder
½ tsp coriander (*dhania*) powder
A pinch turmeric powder (*haldi*)
½ tsp nigella seeds (*kalonji*)
½ tsp chilli powder
2 tsp oil
Salt to taste

To be blended to a tomato purée
½ cup cooked and chopped tomatoes, refer to page 12
¾ tsp fennel seeds (*saunf*)
2 green chillies

1. Combine the oil, fennel seeds, cumin powder, coriander powder, turmeric powder, nigella seeds and chilli powder in a microwave-proof bowl. Mix well and microwave on HIGH for 1 minute.
2. Add the prepared tomato purée, *tindas* and salt and microwave on HIGH for 3 minutes, stirring once in between after 1½ minutes.

Serve hot with rotis.

Karele ki Sukhi Subzi

Here's an interesting way to make karelas without deep-frying them. Stuffed with an array of spices and coated in curds, this truly is a tongue-tickling preparation. If you wish to prepare this subzi for dinner, I suggest you keep the salted karelas aside in the morning to ensure that all the bitterness is removed.

Preparation time: 15 minutes. Cooking time: 13 minutes. Serves 2.

For the *karelas*
4 *karelas* (bitter gourds)
Salt for rubbing

For the filling
1 tsp fennel seeds (*saunf*)
½ cup chopped onions
¼ tsp coriander (*dhania*) powder
¼ tsp chilli powder
A pinch turmeric powder (*haldi*)
¼ tsp *amchur* (dry mango powder)
¼ tsp *garam masala*

2 tsp oil
Salt to taste

To be combined into the curds coating
2 tbsp curds (*dahi*)
1 tbsp milk
¼ tsp chilli powder
¼ tsp *garam masala*
½ tsp ginger paste
Salt to taste

For the *karelas*
1. Peel the *karelas* and slit them lengthwise making sure that they do not separate into two pieces. Carefully remove all the seeds.
2. Rub salt all over and inside the *karelas*. Keep aside for at least 2 to 3 hours.
3. Squeeze out all the water, wash the *karelas* and keep aside.

For the filling
1. Combine the oil and fennel seeds in a microwave-proof bowl and microwave on HIGH for 1 minute.
2. Add the onions, coriander powder, chilli powder, turmeric powder, *amchur*, *garam*

masala, salt and 1 tbsp water. Mix well and microwave on HIGH for 3 minutes, stirring once in between after every 1½ minutes. Keep aside.

How to proceed

1. Stuff the *karelas* with the prepared filling, place them in a microwave-proof plate, sprinkle 1 tbsp water and microwave on HIGH for 5 minutes.
2. Pour the curds coating on them and mix well so that it coats all the karelas.
3. Place the coated *karelas* in a microwave-proof plate and microwave on HIGH for 4 minutes.

   Serve immediately.

Masaledar Aloo Palak

Mashed potatoes and spinach come together with Punjabi chole masala in this easy to make, distinctly flavoured and scrumptious gravy.

Preparation time: 5 to 7 minutes. Cooking time: 5 minutes. Serves 2.

¾ cup cooked and mashed potatoes, refer to page 12
¾ cup cooked spinach (*palak*) purée, refer to page 12
1½ tsp ginger-garlic paste
3 tbsp onion paste
1 tbsp milk
1 tsp chilli powder
1 tsp Punjabi *chole masala*
2 tsp oil
Salt to taste

For the garnish
2 tsp cream

1. Combine the oil, ginger-garlic paste and onion paste in a microwave-proof bowl, cover with a lid and microwave on HIGH for 3 minutes.
2. Add the spinach purée, potatoes, milk, chilli powder, Punjabi *chole masala*, salt and ¼ cup of water, mix well and microwave on HIGH for 2 minutes.
   Serve hot garnished with cream.

Khatte Meethe Kaddu

Tickle your taste buds with this sweet and sour subzi. The versatile pumpkin can be cooked within minutes and makes this an ideal dish to whip up when you are in a hurry.

Preparation time: 5 to 7 minutes. Cooking time: 5 minutes. Serves 2.

1½ cups red pumpkin (*kaddu*), cut into ½″x ½″ cubes
1 tsp fenugreek (*methi*) seeds
1 tsp fennel seeds (*saunf*)
1 tsp cumin seeds (*jeera*)
2 dry red chillies
1 tsp chopped ginger
¼ tsp turmeric powder (*haldi*)
1 tsp coriander (*dhania*) powder
¼ tsp chilli powder
A pinch sugar
2 tsp oil
Salt to taste

For the garnish
1 tsp ginger, cut into thin strips

1. Combine the fenugreek seeds, fennel seeds and cumin seeds in a microwave-proof plate and microwave on HIGH for ½ minute. Coarsely pound the seeds and keep aside.
2. Combine the oil and the coarsely pounded spices in a microwave-proof bowl and microwave on HIGH for 1 minute.
3. Add the dry red chillies and ginger and microwave on HIGH for ½ minute.
4. Add the pumpkin, turmeric powder, coriander powder, chilli powder, sugar and salt and mix well. Microwave on HIGH for 3 minutes till the pumpkin is cooked. Serve hot garnished with ginger.

Masaledar Arbi

The ever-popular arbi is spiked with curds, amchur and other masalas that make this is a peppy delicacy. The secret of making this recipe well lies in choosing the arbis well.

Preparation time: 5 minutes. Cooking time: 4 minutes. Serves 2.

2 cups cooked colocasia (*arbi*), refer to page 13, cut into 12 mm. (½") pieces
1 tbsp ginger-garlic paste
1 tsp finely chopped green chillies
½ tsp lemon juice
½ tsp roughly crushed *ajwain* (carom seeds)
1 tsp oil
Salt to taste

To be mixed into a *masala*
2 tbsp thick curds *(dahi)*
1 tsp *besan* (Bengal gram flour)
1 tsp chopped coriander (*dhania*)
1 tsp chopped mint leaves (*phudina*)
½ tsp chilli powder

½ tsp *garam masala*
¼ tsp *amchur* (dry mango powder)
1 tsp oil

For the garnish
2 tsp chopped coriander

1. Combine the oil, ginger-garlic paste, green chillies, lemon juice, *ajwain* and salt in a microwave-proof bowl and microwave on HIGH for 1 minute.
2. Add the prepared *masala* and colocasia and microwave on HIGH for 3 minutes, stirring once in between, after 1½ minutes.
   Serve hot garnished with coriander.

Khuswale Baingan

Curds and spring onions add zing to this baingan recipe. Teamed with steamed rice it forms a meal that will be fondly remembered by your taste buds.

Preparation time: 10 minutes. Cooking time: 10½ minutes. Serves 2.

4 small brinjals (*baingan*)
½ tsp fenugreek (*methi*) seeds
½ tsp chilli powder
¼ cup fresh curds (*dahi*)
1 tbsp oil
Salt to taste

For the paste
1 tbsp poppy seeds (*khus-khus*)
1 tsp *charoli* (piyal seeds)
1 tsp cumin seeds (*jeera*)
½ cup roughly chopped spring onions
½ tsp chopped green chillies
2 cloves garlic

For the garnish
1 tsp finely chopped spring onion greens

PESHAWARI PANEER : Recipe on page 39. →

For the paste

1. Combine the poppy seeds, *charoli* and cumin seeds in a microwave-proof bowl, cover with a lid and microwave on HIGH for 1½ minutes.
2. Remove and grind to a fine powder in a mixer.
3. Add the spring onions, green chillies and garlic to the mixer and blend to a smooth paste using some water if required. Keep aside.

How to proceed

1. Slit the brinjals lengthwise into four carefully so that they remain joint at the stem. Soak in water to prevent discolouration.
2. Combine the oil and fenugreek seeds in a microwave-proof bowl, cover with a lid and microwave on HIGH for 1 minute.
3. Add the prepared paste, chilli powder and salt, mix well and microwave on HIGH for 3 minutes.
4. Add the curds, slit brinjals and ½ cup water and microwave on HIGH for 5 minutes.

   Serve hot garnished with spring onion greens.

Peshawari Paneer

Picture on page 37.

A rich and creamy mughlai specialty that is laden with cashews and khoya, Peshawari Paneer is best eaten with hot butter naans.

Preparation time: 10 to 12 minutes. Cooking time: 6 minutes. Serves 2.

½ cup *paneer* (cottage cheese), cut into 12 mm. (½") cubes
1 tbsp cashewnuts *(kaju)*
½ tsp chopped ginger
1 tsp finely chopped green chillies
2 tbsp mava (*khoya*)
3 cardamoms (*elaichi*)
2 cloves *(laung / lavang)*
1 tbsp onion paste
A pinch white pepper powder

½ cup milk
1 tbsp cream
A pinch sugar
2 tsp oil
Salt to taste

For the garnish
4 saffron *(kesar)* threads, diluted in 1 tsp water
2 tsp thinly sliced almonds

1. Combine the cashewnuts, ginger, green chillies, mava and 2 cardamoms and blend to a fine paste in a mixer. Keep aside.
2. Combine the oil, the remaining 1 cardamom, cloves and onion paste in a microwave-proof bowl and microwave on HIGH for 3 minutes, stirring once in between after 1½ minutes.
3. Add the prepared paste, mix well and microwave on HIGH for 2 minutes.
4. Add the white pepper powder, milk, sugar and salt and mix well. Add the *paneer* and microwave on HIGH for 1 minute.
5. Add the cream and mix gently.
   Serve hot garnished with saffron and almonds.

Paneer Akuri

Crumbled cottage cheese cooked in tomatoes and spices. A unique Parsi specialty that is very delicious despite being relatively simple and quick-to-make.

Preparation time: 5 to 7 minutes. Cooking time: 7 minutes. Serves 2.

1 cup crumbled *paneer* (cottage cheese)
1 tsp cumin seeds (*jeera*)
1 tsp ginger-garlic paste
¼ cup onion paste
½ cup deseeded and roughly chopped tomatoes
2 tsp finely chopped green chillies
½ tsp turmeric powder (*haldi*)
1 tsp *garam masala*
2 tsp oil
Salt to taste

For the garnish
1 tsp chopped coriander

1. Combine the oil and cumin seeds in a microwave-proof bowl and microwave on HIGH for 1 minute.
2. Add the ginger-garlic paste and onion paste, mix well and microwave on HIGH for 3 minutes, stirring once in between after 1½ minutes.
3. Add the tomatoes, green chillies and turmeric powder, salt and *garam masala,* lightly mash the tomatoes and then microwave on HIGH for 2 minutes.
4. Add the *paneer,* mix well and microwave on HIGH for 1 minute.
   Serve hot garnished with coriander.

Paneer Kalimirch

A brilliant combination of hot peppercorns and mild paneer that is sure to pep you up!

Preparation time: 10 minutes. Cooking time: 3½ minutes. Serves 2.

1 cup *paneer* (cottage cheese), cut into 12 mm. (½") cubes
4 tbsp cream
3 tbsp milk
2 tsp oil
Salt to taste

To be ground to a coarse paste
½ cup chopped onions
3 tbsp cashewnuts *(kaju)*
½ tsp roughly chopped garlic
½ tsp roughly chopped ginger
2 tsp peppercorns

For the garnish
2 tsp cream

1. Combine the oil and the paste in a microwave-proof bowl and microwave on HIGH for 2 minutes.
2. Add the cream, milk and salt, mix well and microwave on HIGH for 30 seconds.
3. Add the *paneer*, mix well and microwave on HIGH for 1 minute.
   Serve hot garnished with cream.

Methi Paneer

Paneer replaces aloo in this quick-to-make and equally tasty variation of the popular methi aloo.

Preparation time: 12 minutes. Cooking time: 7 minutes 10 seconds. Serves 2.

1¼ cups chopped fenugreek (*methi*) leaves
¾ cup *paneer* (cottage cheese), cut into cut into 12 mm. (½") cubes
½ cup sliced onions
½ cup chopped tomatoes
¼ tsp turmeric powder (*haldi*)
¾ tsp chilli powder
A pinch sugar
3 tsp oil
Salt to taste

1. Combine the *paneer,* a pinch of turmeric powder, ¼ tsp chilli powder and 1 tsp of oil in a microwave-proof plate and mix well so that all the *paneer* pieces are coated with the *masalas.*
2. Microwave on HIGH for 40 seconds. Keep aside.

3. Combine the remaining oil and onions in a microwave-proof bowl, cover with a lid and microwave on HIGH for 3 minutes stirring once in between after 1½ minutes.
4. Add the tomatoes, remaining turmeric powder, remaining chilli powder, sugar, salt and 1 tsp water. Cover with a lid and microwave on HIGH for 2 minutes.
5. Add the fenugreek leaves, mix well and microwave on HIGH for 1 minute.
6. Add the cooked *paneer*, mix well and microwave on HIGH for 30 seconds.
   Serve hot.

Badami Paneer

Fresh and soft paneer cubes in a scrumptious almond-based gravy, made colourful and spicy by the addition of tomato purée, dry red chillies and chilli powder. I suggest soaking the dry red chillies and almonds in warm water before using, as this greatly enhances their taste.

Preparation time: 12 minutes. Cooking time: 6 minutes 40 seconds. Serves 2.

¾ cup *paneer* (cottage cheese), cut into 12 mm. (½") cubes
¼ cup ready-made tomato purée
A pinch turmeric powder (*haldi*)
½ tsp chilli powder
¼ tsp *garam masala*
¼ tsp cumin seeds (*jeera*) powder
¼ tsp coriander (*dhania*) powder
1 tbsp cream or milk
A pinch sugar
3 tsp oil
Salt to taste

To be ground to a smooth paste
10 almonds (*badam*)
2 dry red chillies
¼ cup roughly chopped onions
12 mm. (½") piece ginger
½ tsp roughly chopped garlic

For the garnish
½ tbsp ginger juliennes
½ tbsp chopped coriander

1. Combine the *paneer*, turmeric powder, ¼ tsp chilli powder, 1 tsp oil and salt in a microwave-proof plate and mix well. Microwave on HIGH for 40 seconds. Keep aside.
2. Combine the remaining oil and the prepared paste in a microwave-proof bowl, cover with a lid and microwave on HIGH for 3 minutes stirring once in between after 1½ minutes.
3. Add the tomato purée, remaining chilli powder, *garam masala,* cumin powder, coriander powder and salt, mix well and microwave on HIGH for 2 minutes.
4. Add the *paneer,* cream/milk and sugar and microwave on HIGH for 1 minute. Serve hot garnished with ginger and coriander.

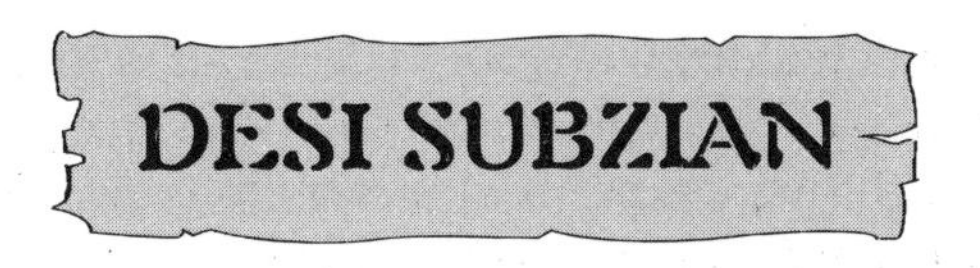

Aloo Poshto

Picture on backcover.

This traditional Bengali speciality is one of my favourite recipes and I recommend that you give this one a try. This recipe proves that poppy seeds and potatoes are a match made in heaven!

Preparation time: 10 minutes. Cooking time: 11½ minutes. Serves 2.

2 cups potato, cut into ½" cubes
2 tbsp poppy seeds (*khus-khus*)
3 dry red chillies, broken into pieces
¼ tsp turmeric powder (*haldi*)
2 tsp oil
Salt to taste

1. Place the poppy seeds on a microwave-proof plate, cover with a lid and microwave on HIGH for 2 minutes. Coarsely grind in a mixer and keep aside.
2. Combine the potatoes with 1 tsp of the oil in another microwave-proof plate and microwave on HIGH for 8 minutes, mixing twice in between. Keep aside.
3. Combine the remaining oil, dry red chillies, turmeric powder and ground poppy seeds in a microwave-proof bowl, mix well and microwave on HIGH for ½ minute.
4. Add the potatoes and salt, mix well and microwave on HIGH for 1 minute.
   Serve hot.

Dahi Bhindi - Kerala Style

The distinct taste of Kerala comes alive in this subtly spiced subzi. The onions and coconut give this gravy a mild crunchy texture and whole red chillies make it a spicy delicacy. Feel free to adjust the amount of chillies to your liking.

Preparation time: 10 minutes. Cooking time: 11 minutes. Serves 2.

12 nos. *bhindi* (ladies fingers), cut into 12mm. (½") pieces
½ tsp cumin seeds (*jeera*)
½ tsp mustard seeds (*rai / sarson*)
3 whole dry red chillies
3 to 4 curry leaves (*kadi patta*)
2 tbsp chopped onions
2 tbsp ready-made tomato purée
½ tsp chilli powder
¼ tsp turmeric powder (*haldi*)
1 tbsp freshly grated coconut
1 tbsp fresh curds (*dahi*)
2 tsp oil
Salt to taste

For the garnish
1 tsp freshly grated coconut

1. Wash the *bhindi* thoroughly and wipe them dry using a cloth and place them in a microwave-proof plate.
2. Sprinkle 1 tsp of oil and 1 tbsp water on the *bhindis* and microwave on HIGH for 4 minutes. Keep aside.
3. Combine the curds with 1 tsp of water in a bowl, whisk well and keep aside.
4. Combine the oil, cumin seeds, mustard seeds, dry red chillies and curry leaves in a microwave-proof bowl, cover with a lid and microwave on HIGH for 1 minute.
5. Add the onions, mix well and microwave on HIGH for 2 minutes.
6. Add the tomato purée, chilli powder, turmeric powder, coconut and salt, mix well and microwave on HIGH for 1 minute.
7. Add the curds and *bhindi,* mix well and microwave on HIGH for 3 minutes stirring once in between after 1½ minutes.

   Serve hot garnished with coconut.

Mirch ka Salan

Picture on page 55.

The traditional hyderabadi salan can now be prepared in the microwave, in just a few minutes and with absolutely no compromise on taste.

Preparation time: 10 to 12 minutes. Cooking time: 8 minutes. Serves 2.

8 long green chillies
½ tsp mustard seeds (*rai / sarson*)
½ nigella seeds (*kalonji*)
½ tsp fenugreek (*methi*) seeds
A pinch asafoetida (*hing*)
¼ tsp turmeric powder (*haldi*)
½ tsp chilli powder
½ tsp ginger-garlic paste
1 tbsp tamarind (*imli*) pulp
3 tsp oil
Salt to taste

For the *masala* paste

1 tbsp chopped dry coconut
1 tbsp poppy seeds (*khus-khus*)
1 tbsp *charoli* (piyal seeds)
1 tbsp sesame seeds (*til*)
1 tbsp peanuts
2 tsp coriander (*dhania*) seeds
3 tsp cumin seeds (*jeera*)
½ tsp oil

For the *masala* paste

1. Combine all the ingredients in a microwave-proof bowl, cover with a lid and microwave on HIGH for 2 minutes stirring once in between after 1 minute.
2. Cool and then grind to a fine paste in a mixer using some water if required. Keep aside.

MIRCH KA SALAN : Recipe on page 53. →

How to proceed

1. Slit each chilli lengthwise taking care that they remain joint at the stem. Remove all seeds and veins.
2. Combine the chillies with 1 tsp oil and mix well so that the oil coats all the chillies. Place them on a microwave-proof plate.
3. Place a glass of water in the centre of the microwave along with the chillies to prevent them from getting wrinkled. Microwave on HIGH for 2 minutes. Keep aside.
4. Combine the remaining oil, mustard seeds, nigella seeds, fenugreek seeds and asafoetida in a microwave-proof bowl, cover with a lid and microwave on HIGH for 1 minute.
5. Add the tumeric powder, chilli powder, ginger-garlic paste, salt, the prepared *masala* paste, ¼ cup water and salt and microwave on HIGH for 2 minutes.
6. Add the slit chillies and tamarind pulp and microwave on HIGH for 1 minute. Serve hot.

Handy tip: Ensure that the *masala* paste if finely ground or it will give the salan a grainy texture.
You can use green Bhavnagri chillies too instead of green chillies.

Goanese Potatoes

This Goanese specialty involves a special cooking method. The masala or paste is pre-cooked and then added to the subzi, thereby giving it a distinct flavour.

Preparation time: 15 minutes.   Cooking time: 5 minutes.   Serves 2.

1 cup cooked and diced potatoes, refer to page 12
½ cup cooked tomato purée, refer to page 12
Salt to taste

For the paste
2 dry red chillies
1 tsp poppy seeds (*khus-khus*)
½ tsp cumin seeds (*jeera*)
1 tsp coriander (*dhania*) seeds
2 tbsp sliced onions
6 mm. (¼") cinnamon (*dalchini*)
2 cloves *(laung / lavang)*
3 peppercorns

3 cloves garlic
2 tbsp freshly grated coconut
2 tsp oil

For the garnish
2 tsp freshly grated coconut

For the paste
1. Combine all the ingredients for the paste in a microwave-proof bowl, cover with a lid and microwave on HIGH for 3 minutes.
2. Allow the mixture to cool and then grind to a smooth paste in a mixer. Keep aside.

How to proceed
1. Combine the prepared paste and the tomato purée in a microwave-proof bowl and microwave on HIGH for 1 minute.
2. Add the potatoes and salt, mix well and microwave on HIGH for 1 minute. Serve hot garnished with coconut.

Baingan Bhurta

Punjabi bhurta just became easier to make! Try this simple microwave recipe for bhurta and have your family licking their fingers tips, and craving for more!

Preparation time: 5 to 7 minutes. Cooking time: 11 minutes. Serves 2.

2 brinjals (*baingan*)
4 tbsp chopped onions
1 tsp chopped green chillies
1 tsp chopped ginger
2 tsp coriander (*dhania*) powder
1 tsp chilli powder
½ tsp turmeric powder (*haldi*)
½ tsp *garam masala*
2 tsp ready-made tomato purée
4 tsp chopped tomatoes
1 tbsp oil
Salt to taste

For the garnish
1 tsp thinly sliced green chillies

1. Place the brinjals on the microwave turnable and microwave on HIGH for 5 minutes. De-skin the brinjals and keep the pulp aside.
2. Combine the oil, onions, green chillies and ginger in a microwave-proof bowl and microwave on HIGH for 3 minutes stirring once in between after 1½ minutes.
3. Add the brinjal pulp, coriander powder, chilli powder, turmeric powder and salt, mix well and microwave on HIGH for 1 minute.
4. Add the *garam masala,* tomato purée and tomatoes, mix well and microwave on HIGH for 2 minutes.

   Serve hot garnished with green chillies.

Kovalam Mutter

A real treat for all green pea lovers! Peas can be cooked within minutes in the microwave, letting you whip up this yummy south Indian style sukhi subzi in no time.

Preparation time: 10 minutes. Cooking time: 3½ minutes. Serves 2.

1 cup cooked green peas, refer to page 13
1 tsp *urad dal* (split black lentils)
½ tsp cumin seeds (*jeera*)
1 tbsp chopped onions
¼ tsp ginger-garlic paste
2 tbsp chopped tomatoes
A pinch turmeric powder (*haldi*)
¼ tsp cumin (*jeera*) powder
½ tsp coriander (*dhania*) powder
½ tsp chilli powder
2 tsp oil
Salt to taste

For the paste
1 tbsp cashewnuts (*kaju*)
2 tbsp roughly chopped coconut

For the garnish
1 tsp chopped coriander

For the paste
1. Combine the cashewnuts and coconut in a microwave-proof plate and microwave on HIGH for 1 minute.
2. Allow to cool and blend with enough water in a mixer to make a thick paste. Keep aside.

How to proceed
1. Combine the oil, *urad dal*, cumin seeds, onions and ginger-garlic paste in a microwave-proof bowl and microwave on HIGH for 1½ minutes.
2. Add the tomatoes, turmeric powder, cumin powder, coriander powder, chilli powder and 2 tsp water, mix well and microwave on HIGH for 1 minute.
3. Add the prepared paste, peas, salt and ¼ cup water, mix well and microwave on HIGH for 1 minute.
   Serve hot garnished with coriander.

Ganthia ki Subzi

Picture on page 65.

A Gujarati specialty, this dish can be prepared even when no veggies are available. Its simplicity and great taste make it one of my favourite preparations. For the perfect experience, add the ganthia just before serving thus preventing it from becoming soggy.

Preparation time: 5 minutes. Cooking time: 3 minutes. Serves 2.

¾ cup *ganthia*
¼ tsp mustard seeds (*rai/ sarson*)
A pinch asafoetida (*hing*)
¼ teaspoon turmeric powder (*haldi*)
¼ tsp chilli powder
2 tbsp fresh curds (*dahi*)
2 tsp oil
Salt to taste

For the garnish
2 tsp chopped coriander
1 tsp *ganthia*

1. Combine the oil and mustard seeds in a microwave-proof bowl, cover with a lid and microwave on HIGH for 1 minute.
2. Add the asafoetida, turmeric powder, chilli powder, curds, salt and ½ cup water, mix well and microwave on HIGH for 2 minutes.
3. Add the *ganthia* and mix well.

   Serve immediately garnished with coriander and *ganthia*.

Variation: ***Muthia ki Subzi***

Instead of *ganthia* you could add *muthias* to the above gravy. For the *muthias* combine 1 cup boiled rice, ¼ cup *besan* (Bengal gram flour), ½ tsp green chilli paste, a pinch asafoetida (*hing*), a pinch turmeric powder (*haldi*), 2 pinches soda-bi-carb, ½ tsp oil and salt to taste in a bowl and mix well. Divide into 15 equal size balls, place them on a microwave-proof plate and microwave on HIGH for 1 minute.

GANTHIA KI SUBZI : Recipe on page 63. →

Bhojpuri Aloo

Traditional Bhojpuri aloo or stuffed potatoes in mouth-watering gravy can be easily prepared in a microwave oven. A well thought out combo of spices ranging from cinnamon to shahjeera, make this a real culinary masterpiece!

Preparation time: 5 to 7 minutes. Cooking time: 7 minutes. Serves 2.

3 cooked potatoes, peeled and halved, refer to page 12
2 cloves (*laung/ lavang*)
1 cardamom (*elaichi*)
1 bayleaf (*tejpatta*)
6 mm. (¼") cinnamon stick (*dalchini*)
½ tsp caraway seeds (*shahjeera*)
¼ tsp ginger-garlic paste
1 tbsp onion paste
¼ tsp turmeric powder (*haldi*)
½ tsp chilli powder
2 tbsp curds (*dahi*)
3 tbsp milk
2 tsp oil

Salt to taste

To be mixed into a stuffing

4 tbsp cooked and mashed potatoes, refer to page 12
A pinch turmeric powder (*haldi*)
½ tsp chilli powder
¼ tsp lemon juice
1 tsp chopped coriander
Salt to taste

For the garnish

2 tsp finely chopped coriander

1. Scoop one half of the potato and stuff with 2 tsp of the stuffing. Repeat for the remaining 5 potato halves. Keep aside.
2. Combine the oil, cloves, cardamom, bayleaf, cinnamon and caraway seeds in a microwave-proof bowl and microwave on HIGH for 2 minutes.
3. Add the ginger-garlic paste, onion paste, turmeric powder, chilli powder and salt, mix well and microwave on HIGH for 2 minutes.
4. Add the curds and milk and mix well microwave on HIGH for 1 minute.
5. Add the stuffed potatoes to the gravy, mix well and microwave on HIGH for 2 minutes.

   Serve hot garnished with coriander.

Sai Bhaji

A staple dish in every Sindhi household, this healthy subzi, loaded with nutritious greens, is the ideal dish to be cooked up in a microwave. The microwave helps retain the colour, flavour and nutrients of the spinach and dill leaves while the potatoes and brinjal add not just volume but also a unique flavour to the subzi.

Preparation time: 10 minutes. Cooking time: 13 minutes. Serves 2.

1 tbsp *chana dal* (split Bengal gram)
2 cups chopped spinach (*palak*)
¾ cup chopped dill (*suva bhaji / shepu*)
½ tsp cumin seeds (*jeera*)
¼ cup finely chopped potatoes
¼ cup finely chopped brinjals (*baingan*)
½ tsp ginger-garlic paste
½ cup cooked and chopped tomatoes, refer to page 12
A pinch turmeric powder (*haldi*)
½ tsp chilli powder
½ tsp coriander (*dhania*) powder
2 tsp oil

Salt to taste

For the garnish
1 tbsp finely chopped tomatoes

1. Combine the *chana dal* with ¼ cup warm water, in a small microwave-proof bowl and let it soak for 30 minutes. Drain and keep aside.
2. Combine the oil and cumin seeds in a microwave-proof bowl and microwave on HIGH for 1 minute.
3. Add the *chana dal*, potatoes, brinjals, ginger-garlic paste and 2 tbsp of water, mix well and microwave on HIGH for 5 minutes.
4. Add the tomatoes, turmeric powder, chilli powder, coriander powder, spinach, dill, salt and ½ cup water. Mix well and microwave on HIGH for 7 minutes. Serve hot garnished with tomatoes.

Hare Mutter ki Curry Mein Aloo

Green peas take on a new avatar, forming the gravy for this innovative dish. Beware, the bowl will be empty even before you know it!

Preparation time: 10 minutes. Cooking time: 3 minutes. Serves 2.

½ cup cooked green peas purée, refer to page 13
¼ cup cooked and diced potatoes, refer to page 12
½ tsp finely chopped green chillies
¼ tsp finely chopped ginger
2 tbsp ready-made tomato purée
1 tbsp finely chopped tomatoes
½ tsp Punjabi *chole masala*
1 tbsp oil
Salt to taste

For the garnish
1 tsp chopped coriander

1. Combine the oil, green peas purée, green chillies and ginger in a microwave-proof bowl and microwave on HIGH for 2 minutes.
2. Add the tomato purée, tomatoes, Punjabi *chole masala*, potatoes, salt and 4 tbsp water, mix well and microwave on HIGH for 1 minute.
   Serve hot garnished with coriander.

Vegetable Korma

Picture on cover.

Need to whip up a party fare within short notice? This quick-to-prepare, tasty and rich recipe is the perfect choice. A simple and tasty microwave version of vegetable korma, this is best eaten with hot parathas.

Preparation time: 10 minutes. Cooking time: 3½ minutes. Serves 2.

1 cup mixed cooked vegetables (carrots, french beans, green peas, cauliflower etc.), refer to page 14
½ cup *paneer* (cottage cheese), cut into 12 mm. (½") cubes
1 tbsp onion paste
½ tsp ginger-garlic paste
¼ tsp turmeric powder (*haldi*)
¼ tsp chilli powder
½ tsp coriander (*dhania*) powder
1 tbsp ready-made tomato purée
½ cup milk
1 tbsp fresh cream

2 tsp oil
Salt to taste

1. Combine the *paneer* with ½ cup water and ½ tsp salt in a microwave-proof bowl and microwave on HIGH for 1 minute. Keep aside.
2. Combine the oil, onion paste and ginger-garlic paste in another microwave-proof bowl, mix well. Cover with a lid and microwave on HIGH for 1 minute.
3. Add the turmeric powder, chilli powder, coriander powder and tomato purée, mix well and microwave on HIGH for 30 seconds.
4. Add the cooked vegetables, milk, 1 tbsp of cream, *paneer* and salt, mix well and microwave on HIGH for 1 minute.
5. Just before serving, top with the remaining cream and serve hot.

Khumbh Lajawab

Picture on facing page.

Kasuri methi bestows a classic flavour to this subzi, which is prepared with mushrooms and a delectable combination of spices. It is a perfect accompaniment for hot rotis or bread.

Preparation time: 5 to 7 minutes. Cooking time: 5 minutes. Serves 2.

1 cup mushrooms (*khumbh*), cut into quarters
1 tbsp onion paste
½ tsp ginger-garlic paste
1 tbsp ready-made tomato purée
¼ tsp cumin seeds (*jeera*) powder
¼ tsp coriander (*dhania*) powder
A pinch turmeric powder (*haldi*)
¼ tsp chilli powder
½ tsp dried fenugreek leaves (*kasuri methi*)
1 tbsp cream
1 tbsp milk
A pinch sugar
2 tsp oil

KHUMBH LAJAWAB : Recipe above. →

Salt to taste

1. Combine the oil, onion paste and ginger-garlic paste in a microwave-proof bowl and microwave on HIGH for 2 minutes.
2. Add the tomato purée, cumin powder, coriander powder, turmeric powder, chilli powder and dried fenugreek leaves, mix well and microwave on HIGH for 1 minute.
3. Add the cream, milk, sugar, salt, mushrooms and 1 tbsp water, mix well and microwave on HIGH for 2 minutes.
   Serve hot.

Mava Mutter

Mutter comes together with mava in this truly royal recipe. Cooked in a blend of carefully chosen spices, this is certainly a meal fit for a king... the food of the maharajas cooked in the microwave!!

Preparation time: 5 minutes. Cooking time: 4½ minutes. Serves 2.

½ cup cooked green peas, refer to page 13
½ cup mava *(khoya)*
½ cup chopped tomatoes
2 cloves (*laung / lavang*)
A pinch asafoetida (*hing*)
¼ tsp coriander *(dhania)* powder
¼ tsp cumin seeds (*jeera*) powder
½ tsp chilli powder
½ tsp finely chopped green chillies
½ tsp dry ginger powder (*soonth)*
½ tsp sugar
1 tsp ready-made tomato purée
2 tsp oil

Salt to taste

1. Combine the oil, cloves and asafoetida in a microwave-proof bowl, cover with a lid and microwave on HIGH for ½ minute.
2. Add the mava and microwave on HIGH for 1 minute.
3. Add the coriander powder, cumin powder, chilli powder, green chillies, dry ginger powder, salt and 1 tbsp water, mix well and microwave on HIGH for 1 minute.
4. Add the sugar, tomato purée, green peas and tomatoes and mix well. Microwave on HIGH for 2 minutes.
   Serve hot.

Baby Corn Masala

Baby corn, sliced onions and capsicum literally play together in this attractive, mouth-watering and crunchy dry subzi. Using coloured capsicums greatly enhances the visual appeal of this dish.

Preparation time: 5 minutes.   Cooking time: 9 minutes.   Serves 2.

1 cup baby corn, cut into half lengthwise
½ tsp *ajwain* (carom seeds), roughly crushed
¼ cup sliced onions
A pinch turmeric powder (*haldi*)
¼ tsp chilli powder
¼ tsp *garam masala*
2 cardamoms (*elaichi*), crushed
¼ cup sliced capsicum (yellow, red, green)
¼ cup sliced tomatoes
2 tsp oil
Salt to taste

For the garnish
1 tbsp chopped coriander

1. Combine the oil and *ajwain* in a microwave-proof bowl and microwave on HIGH for 1 minute.
2. Add the onions, mix well and microwave on HIGH for 2 minutes.
3. Add the baby corn and 1 tbsp water, mix well and microwave on HIGH for 3 minutes.
4. Add the turmeric powder, chilli powder, *garam masala*, cardamoms, capsicum, tomatoes and salt and mix well. Microwave on HIGH for 3 minutes.
   Serve hot garnished with coriander.

Darbari Subzi

Picture on page 1.

Ever tried adding cashewnuts and raisins to the traditional aloo mutter? Here is an interesting recipe that whips up such a combination! There is an exciting burst of flavour in every bite.

Preparation time: 5 to 7 minutes.   Cooking time: 10 minutes.   Serves 2.

1 cup cooked and diced potatoes, refer to page 12
½ cup cooked green peas, refer to page 13
2 tsp sesame seeds (*til*)
½ tsp cumin seeds (*jeera*)
¼ cup onion rings
1 tbsp cashewnuts (*kaju*)
2 tsp raisins (*kismis*)
⅓ cup ready-made tomato purée
¼ tsp *garam masala*
¼ tsp turmeric powder (*haldi*)
½ tsp chilli powder
1 tbsp milk
A pinch sugar

2 tsp oil
Salt to taste

For the garnish
1 tbsp chopped coriander

1. Place the sesame seeds on a microwave-proof plate and microwave on HIGH for 1 minute. Keep aside.
2. Combine the oil, cumin seeds and onions in another microwave-proof bowl and microwave on HIGH for 3 minutes.
3. Add the cashewnuts, raisins and 1 tbsp water, mix well and microwave on HIGH for 2 minutes.
4. Add the tomato purée, *garam masala,* turmeric powder and chilli powder, mix well and microwave on HIGH for 2 minutes.
5. Add the potatoes, green peas, sesame seeds, sugar and salt, mix well and microwave on HIGH for 1 minute.
6. Add the milk, stir once and microwave on HIGH for 1 minute.
   Serve hot garnished with coriander.

Baghara Tamatar

Picture on page 85.

Surprise your guests with this innovative dish made with a combination of chopped tomatoes and tomato purée.

Preparation time: 10 minutes. Cooking time: 10 minutes. Serves 2.

1 cup chopped tomatoes
¼ cup cooked tomato purée, refer to page 12
½ tsp nigella seeds (*kalongi*)
½ tsp mustard seeds (*rai / sarson*)
¼ tsp coriander (*dhania*) seeds
2 tbsp chopped onions
4 to 5 curry leaves (*kadi patta*)
¼ tsp turmeric powder (*haldi*)
¼ tsp chilli powder
2 tsp oil
Salt to taste

For the powder
1 tbsp sesame seeds (*til*)

1 tbsp peanuts
1 tbsp chopped dried coconut

For the powder

1. Combine all the ingredients in a microwave-proof bowl and microwave on HIGH for 3 minutes stirring once in between after every 1½ minutes.
2. Remove, cool and grind to a powder in a mixer. Keep aside.

How to proceed

1. Combine the oil, nigella seeds, mustard seeds and coriander seeds and microwave on HIGH for 2 minutes.
2. Add the onions and curry leaves, mix well and microwave on HIGH for 2 minutes.
3. Add the prepared powder, tomatoes, tomato purée, turmeric powder, chilli powder, salt and 1 tbsp water, mix well. Cover with a lid and microwave on HIGH for 3 minutes.

   Serve hot with steamed rice or pulao.

BAGHARA TAMATAR: Recipe on page 83. →

Soya aur Gobhi ki Bhaji

Try this tasty bhaji, which is made with healthy soya granules and grated cauliflower, cooked in the microwave. It tastes best when eaten steaming hot.

Preparation time: 10 minutes. Cooking time: 6 minutes. Serves 2.

2 tbsp soya granules
½ cup grated cauliflower
2 tbsp onion paste
½ tsp ginger-garlic paste
½ tsp cumin seeds (*jeera*) powder
½ tsp coriander (*dhania*) powder
¼ tsp chilli powder
¼ tsp turmeric powder (*haldi*)
2 tbsp ready-made tomato purée
2 tbsp milk
1 tbsp oil
Salt to taste

For the garnish
2 tsp chopped coriander

1. Combine the soya granules with ¼ cup warm water in a bowl and soak for 15 to 20 minutes till soft. Drain and keep aside.
2. Combine the oil, onion paste and ginger-garlic paste in a microwave-proof bowl and microwave on HIGH for 2 minutes.
3. Add the cumin powder, coriander powder, chilli powder, turmeric powder and 1 tsp water, mix well and microwave on HIGH for 1 minute.
4. Add the tomato purée, soya granules, cauliflower, milk, salt and ¼ cup water, mix well and microwave on HIGH for 3 minutes.

   Serve hot garnished with coriander.

Spicy Corn Palak

This spicy combination of corn and palak is a delight to behold and to taste! Indeed, a rare combination of beauty and flavour.

Preparation time: 5 to 7 minutes. Cooking time: 5 minutes. Serves 2.

¾ cup blanched spinach (*palak*), refer to page 12
¼ cup cooked corn niblets, refer to page 13
¼ cup chopped onions
½ tsp chopped green chillies
¼ tsp chopped garlic
¼ tsp chopped ginger
2 tbsp ready-made tomato purée
¼ tsp chilli powder
½ tsp Punjabi *chole masala*
1 tbsp milk
2 tsp oil
Salt to taste

1. Combine the oil, onions, green chillies, garlic and ginger in a microwave-proof bowl and microwave on HIGH for 3 minutes.
2. Add the tomato purée, chilli powder, Punjabi *chole masala*, milk, salt, spinach and corn, mix well and microwave on HIGH for 2 minutes.
   Serve hot.

Makai Kofta aur Hariyali Curry

America meets India. Grated American corn dumplings in a coconut milk and coriander flavoured gravy, which is sure to tickle and tease your gastronomic senses!

Preparation time: 5 minutes. Cooking time: 6½ minutes. Serves 2.

For the *makai koftas*
¼ cup grated corn (*makai / bhutta)*
2 tbsp rice flour (*chawal ka atta*)
2 tsp chopped coriander
½ tsp chopped green chillies
Salt to taste

For the *hariyali* curry
1 tsp ginger-garlic paste

6 mm. (¼") piece cinnamon (*dalchini*)
2 cardamoms (*elaichi*)
2 cloves (*laung/ lavang*)
½ cup coconut milk
½ tsp cornflour mixed with ¼ cup water
2 tsp oil
Salt to taste

To be ground into the *hariyali* paste
1 cup roughly chopped coriander (*dhania*)
1 tbsp lime juice
3 green chillies

For the garnish
2 tsp cream

For the *makai koftas*
1. Mix all the ingredients for the *koftas* with 1 tsp of water and make a thick dough.
2. Divide the mixture into 6 equal portions and shape into small balls.
3. Gently place the balls on a microwave-proof plate and microwave on HIGH for 30 seconds. Keep aside.

For the *hariyali* curry

1. Combine the oil, ginger-garlic paste, cinnamon, cardamom and cloves in a microwave-proof bowl, cover with a lid and microwave on HIGH for 1 minute.
2. Add the *hariyali* paste, mix well and microwave on HIGH for 2 minutes.
3. Add the coconut milk, cornflour mixture and salt, mix well and microwave on HIGH for 2 minutes.

How to proceed

Just before serving, gently add the *koftas* to the curry and microwave on HIGH for 1 minute.

Serve hot garnished with cream.

Laknavi Kofta Curry

Picture on page 2.

Would you believe it if I said koftas can be prepared without deep frying? Koftas can be prepared in the microwave without frying, and they taste just as good as the original! Enjoy these soft koftas made with potatoes, spinach and fenugreek leaves and ensure good health.

Preparation time: 15 minutes. Cooking time: 5½ minutes. Serves 2.

For the *koftas*
½ cup cooked and mashed potatoes, refer to page 12
1 tbsp chopped coriander
1 tbsp chopped fenugreek (*methi*) leaves
1 tbsp chopped spinach *(palak)*
1 tsp lemon juice
1 tsp finely chopped green chillies
½ tsp cornflour
2 tbsp milk
Salt to taste

To be ground to a smooth paste
½ tbsp poppy seeds (*khus-khus*)
1 tbsp cashewnuts (*kaju*)
2 green chillies
1 tbsp water

For the curry
2 tbsp onion paste
½ tsp ginger-garlic paste
¼ cup curds (*dahi*)
¼ cup milk
½ tsp cornflour mixed with 2 tsp water
A pinch turmeric powder (*haldi*)
2 tsp oil
Salt to taste

For the garnish
2 tbsp chopped coriander

For the *koftas*
1. Combine all the ingredients in a bowl and mix well to form a soft dough.

2. Divide the dough into 8 equal portions and place them on a microwave-proof plate and microwave on HIGH for 30 seconds. Keep aside.

For the curry

1. Combine the oil, onion paste and ginger-garlic paste in a microwave-proof bowl and microwave on HIGH for 2 minutes.
2. Add the prepared paste, mix well and microwave on HIGH for 1 minute.
3. Add the curds, milk, cornflour mixture, turmeric powder and salt, mix well and microwave on HIGH for 1 minute.

How to proceed

Combine the curry and the *koftas* and microwave on HIGH for 1 minute.
Serve immediately garnished with coriander.

South Indian Baby Corn Curry

Baby corn in a delicious curry form, flavoured subtly and aesthetically with a blend of south Indian spices.

Preparation time: 10 minutes. Cooking time: 7 minutes. Serves 2.

12 to 15 baby corns, cut into halves
½ cup tamarind (*imli*) water
½ tsp mustard seeds (*rai/ sarson*)
½ tsp cumin seeds (*jeera*)
¼ tsp asafoetida (*hing*)
½ tsp finely chopped garlic
½ tsp finely chopped ginger
1 tsp coriander (*dhania*) powder
¼ tsp turmeric powder (*haldi*)
1 tsp chilli powder
½ tsp curry powder
½ tsp sugar
2 tsp oil

Salt to taste

1. Combine the baby corn with 2 tbsp water in a microwave proof plate and microwave on HIGH for 2 minutes. Keep aside.
2. Combine the oil, mustard seeds, cumin seeds and asafoetida in a microwave-proof bowl, cover with a lid and microwave on HIGH for 1 minute.
3. Add the garlic and ginger, mix well and cover with a lid and microwave on HIGH for 1 minute.
4. Add the tamarind water, coriander powder, turmeric powder, chilli powder, curry powder, sugar and salt, mix well and microwave on HIGH for 2 minutes stirring once in between after 1 minute.
5. Add the baby corn, mix well and microwave on HIGH for 1 minute.
   Serve hot with steamed rice.

Corn Curry

A quick curry made with grated corn, coconut milk and spices. You could also add any pre-cooked vegetables to this curry. This curry combines beautifully with steaming hot rice or vegetable idlis.

Preparation time: 10 minutes. Cooking time: 4 minutes. Serves 2.

1/3 cup grated sweet corn
1/4 tsp cumin seeds (*jeera*)
A pinch asafoetida (*hing*)
1 tbsp onion paste
1 tbsp ready-made tomato purée
1/2 tsp curry powder
1/2 cup coconut milk
2 tsp oil
Salt to taste

For serving
Vegetable idlis or
Steamed rice

1. Combine the oil and cumin seeds in a microwave-proof bowl, cover with a lid and microwave on HIGH for 1 minute till the seeds crackle.
2. Add the asafoetida and onion paste, mix well and microwave on HIGH for 1 minute.
3. Add the corn, tomato purée, curry powder, coconut milk, salt and 1/2 cup water, mix well and microwave on HIGH for 2 minutes.
   Serve hot with vegetable idlis or steamed rice.

Zaykedaar Subzi

This is certainly a no-hassle subzi… just toss in all the ingredients and let the microwave work its magic.

Preparation time: 10 minutes. Cooking time: 5 minutes. Serves 2.

1 cup mixed chopped vegetables (potatoes, cauliflower, peas, carrots)
½ tsp chilli powder
A pinch turmeric powder (*haldi*)
½ tsp coriander (*dhania*) powder
½ tsp cumin seeds (*jeera*) powder
¼ tsp *garam masala*
2 tbsp oil
Salt to taste

To be ground into a paste
¼ cup fresh grated coconut
1 medium onion
1 tsp chopped green chillies
12 mm. (½") piece ginger
5 small cloves garlic

1. Combine the oil, the prepared paste, chilli powder, turmeric powder, coriander powder, cumin powder, *garam masala,* mixed vegetables, salt and ¼ cup water in a microwave-proof bowl, mix well and microwave on HIGH for 3 minutes.
2. Stir once and microwave on HIGH for 2 minutes. Serve hot.

Malai Kofta Curry

A simple yet flavourful tomato-based curry takes on a rich form with the addition of potato and cottage cheese koftas stuffed with dry fruits.

Preparation time: 15 minutes. Cooking time: 6 minutes. Serves 2.

For the *koftas*
½ cup cooked and mashed potatoes, refer to page 12
¼ cup *paneer* (cottage cheese)
1 tsp finely chopped green chillies
1 tbsp finely chopped coriander
2 tbsp milk
5 cashewnuts *(kaju),* cut into halves
10 raisins (*kismis*)
Salt to taste

For the curry
1 tbsp ready-made tomato purée
1 tsp cornflour diluted in 2 tbsp milk
A pinch sugar

1 tbsp oil
Salt to taste

To be ground to a smooth paste
1 tbsp fresh grated coconut
2 tbsp roughly copped onions
2 dry red chillies
1 tsp coriander (*dhania*) seeds
½ tsp cumin seeds (*jeera*)
1 tsp poppy seeds (*khus-khus*)
½ tsp ginger-garlic paste
1 tsp chopped coriander
1 tbsp *charoli* (piyal seeds)
¼ cup water

For the garnish
1 tbsp fresh cream
½ tbsp grated cheese

For the *koftas*

1. Combine the potatoes, *paneer*, coriander, chillies, milk and salt in a bowl and mix well to form a soft dough.
2. Divide the dough into 10 equal sized portions and keep aside.
3. In 1 portion of the dough stuff ½ a cashewnut and 1 raisin and shape it into a small ball.
4. Repeat for the remaining 9 portions.
5. Place them on a microwave-proof plate and microwave on HIGH for 1 minute. Keep aside.

For the curry

1. Combine the oil, the prepared paste, tomato purée, cornflour-milk mixture, sugar and ¾ cup water, in a microwave-proof bowl and microwave on HIGH for 3 minutes.
2. Add the *koftas* and microwave on HIGH for 2 minutes.
   Serve hot garnished with cream and cheese.